WHY DO MY EYES ITCH?

+ and other questions about allergies +

Heinemann
LIBRARY

Angela Royston

www.heinemann.co.uk/library
Visit our website to find out more information about **Heinemann Library** books.

To order:
☎ Phone 44 (0) 1865 888066
🗎 Send a fax to 44 (0) 1865 314091
💻 Visit the Heinemann Bookshop at www.heinemann.co.uk/library to browse our catalogue and order online.

First published in Great Britain by Heinemann Library, Halley Court, Jordan Hill, Oxford OX2 8EJ, a division of Reed Educational and Professional Publishing Ltd. Heinemann is a registered trademark of Reed Educational & Professional Publishing Limited.

OXFORD MELBOURNE AUCKLAND JOHANNESBURG BLANTYRE
GABORONE IBADAN PORTSMOUTH NH (USA) CHICAGO

Designed by Joanna Sapwell and StoryBooks
Illustrations by Nick Hawken
Originated by Ambassador Litho Ltd
Printed in China by South China Printing Company

ISBN 0 431 11071 9
06 05 04 03 02
10 9 8 7 6 5 4 3 2 1

British Library Cataloguing in Publication Data
Royston, Angela
Why do my eyes itch?.– (Body matters)
1. Eye – Juvenile literature 2. Itching – Juvenile literature
I.Title
612.8'4

Acknowledgements
The Publishers would like to thank the following for permission to reproduce photographs:
Bsip: 18; Corbis: 19, 27; Gareth Boden: 14, 15, 20, 21, 22; Mike Wyndham: 13; PA Photos: 4; Science Photo Library/Dr Jeremy Burgess: 16; Science Photo Library/Mike Bluestone: 24; Science Photo Library/Simon Fraser: 25; Science Photo Library: 5, 6, 7, 8, 9, 11, 12, 17, 23, 26, 28.

Cover photograph reproduced with permission of Tudor Photography.

Our thanks to Anne Long for her help in the preparation of this book.

Every effort has been made to contact copyright holders of any material reproduced in this book. Any omissions will be rectified in subsequent printings if notice is given to the Publisher.

CONTENTS

Words printed in **bold letters like these** are explained in the Glossary.

WHAT IS AN ALLERGY?

An allergy occurs when the body thinks that something is harmful to it, although the same thing is harmless to most people. For example, some people are very **sensitive** to peanuts. If they eat anything with peanuts in, their bodies treat the peanuts as harmful **germs**.

The body's defences

The body has several ways of defending itself from things that harm it. White blood **cells** attack and destroy dirt and germs. And, when a new kind of germ enters the body, the blood makes a special kind of cell, called an **antibody**, to attack it. It makes a different antibody for each kind of germ.

This girl is very unlucky. She is allergic to so many things she has to live inside this special tent.

Histamine

When part of the body is damaged, it releases a chemical called **histamine**. Histamine allows blood to flood the damaged area, bringing extra white blood cells and antibodies to fight any invaders. The extra blood can also make that area of the body red or swollen.

Allergic reaction

Something that causes an **allergy** is called an **allergen**. When someone is allergic to something, their blood makes antibodies against it. As soon as the antibodies detect the allergen their body releases histamine. The histamine can make them sneeze and their nose run. It may make their skin red and itchy. It can even make them vomit. Drugs called **antihistamines** stop histamine working in the body and are often used to treat allergies.

COMMON CAUSES OF ALLERGIES:

- pollen
- dust mites
- feathers
- cat hair
- mould
- soap powder
- certain foods.

This is what histamine looks like under a microscope. When you are allergic to something, your body produces too much histamine. It can affect your breathing or make you vomit.

WHY DO MY EYES ITCH?

Your eyes itch when something irritates the inside of your eyelids. If a large speck of dust blows into your eye, your eye hurts, but smaller specks may make your eyes itch. Tiny specks include **germs**, cigarette smoke and other kinds of air pollution. If you are allergic to something, such as pollen, that makes your eyes itch too.

Eye wash

A film of salty water covers each eye and helps to keep it moist and clean. Every time you blink, your eyelid washes your eye like a windscreen wiper. When something irritates your eye, your body makes extra salty water to wash it out.

This boy's eyelids are red and swollen because he is allergic to pollen. It also makes his eyes water and his eyelids itchy.

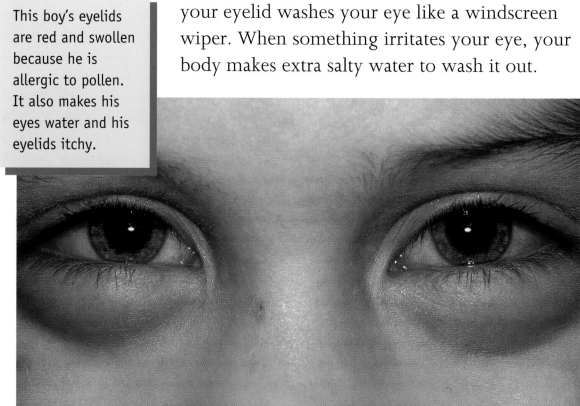

Swollen eyelids

If your eyelids are allergic to something, your body releases **histamine**. This makes your eyelids red and swollen and your eyes itchy. Taking **antihistamine** will help to reduce the effects. Infections, such as conjunctivitis, also make your eyelids red and swollen.

If you are allergic to cigarette smoke, it will make your eyes itchy and sore and your eyelids swollen.

IRRITATING SPECKS

- Pollen is a very fine dust that flowers make.
- Germs are too small to be seen. Each kind of germ makes you ill in a different way. One germ that makes your eyes itch causes conjunctivitis. Another germ causes styes.
- Millions of tiny specks of dirt float through the air. Most are too small to see. They are made by cars, trucks and factories.
- Cigarette smoke is tiny specks of burnt tobacco.

WHAT IS HAYFEVER?

Suffering from hayfever is like having a cold for weeks on end. People with hayfever sneeze, their noses run all the time and their eyes are red and itchy. Their face may become puffy and they feel ill. Hayfever is caused by an **allergy** to pollen.

Grasses have small, green flowers that produce lots of pollen. Here, the clusters of fine yellow dust have been magnified.

What is pollen?

Pollen is a fine, yellow powder that flowers produce in order to make new seeds. To make a new seed, a single grain of male pollen joins with the female sex **cell** of another flower. Some kinds of plants, particularly grasses and trees, rely on the wind to blow their pollen from one flower to another, but in the process the grains of pollen float far and wide.

Pollen count

In early summer, weather reports often give a pollen count as a figure out of ten. The higher the figure the more pollen there is in the air. Different plants produce pollen at particular times of the spring and summer, but most produce it in late spring and early summer.

Trapped indoors

People who suffer from hayfever try to avoid going near grass and flowers when the pollen count is high. This means that they have to keep out of their gardens in early summer. Many hayfever sufferers also take **antihistamine** to reduce their symptoms.

This girl suffers from hayfever. When she breathes pollen in the air into her nose, it makes her sneeze.

HOW DO ALLERGIES AFFECT BREATHING?

Feathers, wool, pet hairs, dust and dust mites all produce fine grains or powders. Like pollen, the fine grains float in the air and can cause **allergies** that affect breathing.

An allergy can affect any part of the body that the air you breathe in reaches – particularly the nose and the bronchial tubes.

What happens to the air you breathe in?

When you breathe in, air passes through your nose and mouth into the **bronchial tubes** and then to thinner tubes in your lungs. All of these breathing tubes are lined with fine hairs and **mucus** to catch any dirt, **germs** or dust that you breathe in with the air. Inside your lungs, oxygen from the air passes into the blood, and waste carbon dioxide (gas in the air) leaves the blood to join the air that is breathed out.

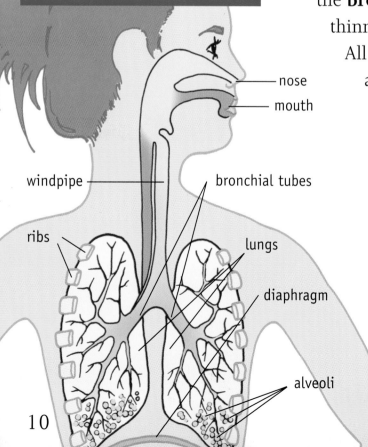

nose
mouth
windpipe
bronchial tubes
ribs
lungs
diaphragm
alveoli

Allergic reaction

People often sneeze or cough when they breathe in an **allergen**. This is the body's way of getting rid of dust in the nose or throat. The nose also produces extra mucus to help wash it away. Some people only react to an allergen when it reaches their lungs. Then the body produces **histamine** that makes the bronchial tubes become narrower and even close up. This can make it difficult to breathe in and out.

Pets make some people sneeze or cough. Cats that have fleas and dandruff are more likely to cause allergies.

Asthma

People who have **asthma** also find it difficult to breathe. During an attack, their bronchial tubes become tight and they make a wheezing sound as they breathe. An attack may last a few minutes or much longer. An allergy is a common cause of an asthma attack although there are many other causes too.

Avoiding allergens

Some **allergens** are easier to avoid than others. If you are allergic to feathers, then you can use a pillow and duvet made of **synthetic materials**. If you are allergic to wool, then you can wear clothes that have no wool in them. And if you are allergic to cats or dogs, then you should not keep them as pets.

Avoiding dust and dust mites

Dust is harder to avoid. Most of the dust in your home is made of tiny flakes of dead skin. If you are allergic to dust, it is helpful to vacuum clean

Dust mites are tiny insects that are too small to see without a microscope. This is what a dust mite looks like when it is magnified.

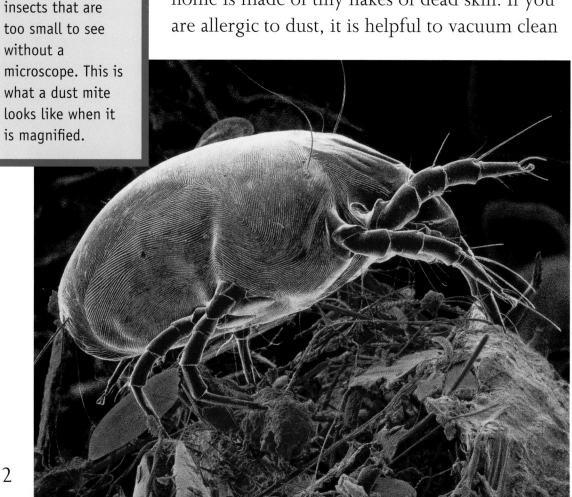

12

all the floors and your bedding every day. Dust mites feed on dust. They are so small they pass straight through most vacuum cleaners, but some cleaners have a special filter for catching tiny grains of dust and dust mites. Carpets collect dust, so you may have to do without them.

Antihistamine

Antihistamines are drugs that reduce the symptoms of an **allergy**, but they are not a cure. When antihistamine tablets are taken regularly, they work for a long period of time. Antihistamine can also be sprayed or dropped directly into the nose. This gives quick relief for a short time, but can damage the delicate lining inside the nose if used over many years.

This girl is using an inhaler that contains an antihistamine because she is very allergic to dust. The antihistamine reduces the symptoms of the allergy.

ALLERGY SUFFERERS

About one in every three people in Britain and one in every five in the United States suffers from an allergy.

13

WHY DOES MY SKIN ITCH?

Some **allergies** affect the skin. If you have **sensitive** skin, **biological detergents**, and scented soaps and cosmetics, may make your skin itch. People with sensitive skin may have to buy pure soap, non-biological soap powders and non-allergenic cosmetics.

Sun allergy

Some people are allergic to the Sun. Their skin comes up in small blisters unless they wear long-sleeved clothes and trousers and avoid strong sunshine. Everyone should protect their skin against damage from the Sun's rays, by wearing a shirt and sunhat and rubbing sun protection cream into their skin.

People with sensitive skins have to be careful which detergent they use to wash their clothes and which soaps and creams they use on their skin.

Food allergies

Many people are allergic to strawberries, nuts or other foods. If they eat something with nuts in, for example, their skin may become red and blotchy. Their skin feels very uncomfortable for a few hours until the allergy dies down.

Other itchy things

Having itchy skin does not mean that you must have an allergy. Many people find that rough cloth or fluffy wool, such as mohair, feels itchy against their skin. Most rashes are itchy too, particularly heat rash and the rash caused by chickenpox. Dabbing on camomile lotion or a solution of sodium bicarbonate helps to soothe the itching.

Try not to scratch if you have a condition such as chickenpox, eczema or an allergy. Scratching may make your skin red and sore.

THINGS THAT CAN MAKE YOUR SKIN ITCH

Many different things can cause skin allergies if you are allergic to them. They include:

- soap and detergents
- eating strawberries, shellfish, eggs, milk, nuts
- insect bites and stings
- eczema
- medicines such as aspirin and penicillin
- stinging nettles.

Stings and bites

When an insect such as a bee or wasp stings you, it injects poison into your blood. Your body's natural defence to a sting is to produce **histamine**. Histamine makes the skin around the sting swell up and become red and itchy.

Insect bites

Some insects, such as mosquitoes and head lice, bite animals and people in order to feed on their blood. As a mosquito stabs your skin with its mouth, some of its saliva runs into the wound. The saliva stops your blood clotting so that the mosquito can suck up more blood. But most people are allergic to the mosquito's saliva. Their body produces histamine and it makes the bite red and itchy.

When a bee or wasp stings you, it often leaves its sting in your skin. Pull the sting out very carefully.

Treating insect stings and bites

Antihistamine cream helps to stop stings and bites from hurting and itching. But if you have caught head lice, the only way to stop your scalp from itching is to get rid of the lice. To do this you need to use a special shampoo or lotion that you can buy from the chemists. Scabies is a very itchy skin condition. It is caused by a tiny mite that burrows beneath the skin. It needs to be treated by a doctor.

STINGING INSECTS

bees, wasps, hornets, ants

BITING INSECTS

mosquitoes, biting midges, gnats, fleas, head lice

Extreme shock

A few people are so allergic to insect bites their bodies go into **extreme shock**. If this happens, get medical help at once.

This is a mosquito. Mosquitos bite people and animals to feed on their blood.

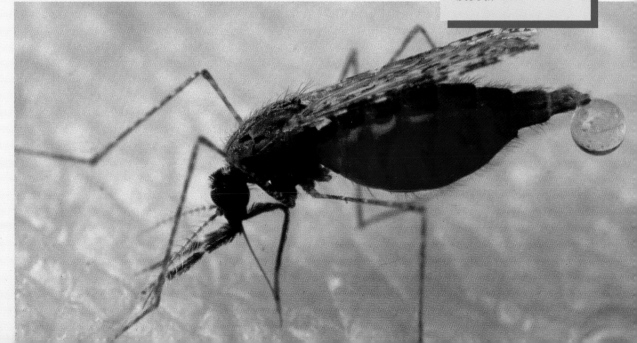

IS ECZEMA CATCHING?

Eczema is a condition that makes the skin dry, swollen and itchy. Sometimes little spots and blisters form that may become crusty when they burst. Eczema may occur on any part of the body, but is common on the elbows and behind the knees. There are several kinds of eczema, none of which is catching. One kind tends to run in families. It is common among young children, but they have often grown out of it by the time they are four years old.

This boy has eczema on the back of his knees. It is important not to scratch eczema because scratching makes it worse.

Allergic eczema

Another kind of eczema is caused by an allergic reaction to something the person touches. This is called contact eczema. Different things cause contact eczema in different people. It is often triggered by plants, cosmetics, medicines and foods that include wheat or milk. People who have allergic eczema often suffer from hayfever or **asthma** too.

Allergies from work

Some people are allergic to chemicals and other things that they touch at work. Some photographers, for example, are allergic to the chemicals that are used to develop photographs. Some bakers and grocers are allergic to foods that they have to touch, and people who work with tar may be allergic to it.

Treating allergic eczema

The best way to treat allergic eczema is to try to avoid the things that trigger it. Using special oils to clean the skin is more soothing than using soap and water. Special creams can also help to reduce the swelling and itching.

Some people find that swimming in the sea can help to reduce eczema. Sunshine can trigger eczema but it usually makes it better.

WHY DO PEANUTS MAKE SOME PEOPLE SICK?

This girl has just eaten some nuts by mistake and is feeling very sick. People who are allergic to nuts often react very quickly to them.

Many people are allergic to peanuts or other nuts, such as pecans and walnuts. Eating even a small amount of peanuts can make them vomit. Vomiting is the body's way of getting rid of something poisonous that you have eaten. So if someone is allergic to nuts, their body reacts as if the nuts were poisonous.

Avoiding nuts

Some people are allergic to just one or two foods. Other people are allergic to many. Avoiding certain foods, such as nuts, is not as easy as it sounds. Many kinds of foods contain small amounts of nuts, including many cereal bars.

Some people are extremely **sensitive** to even tiny amounts of a particular food. The fact that a machine in a factory previously processed nuts is enough to trigger the **allergy**. That is why many products say 'may contain traces of nuts' on the label.

Other symptoms of food allergy

If you eat something that you are allergic to, your mouth may tingle and your lips, tongue and throat may swell up and go numb. It may also give you stomach ache and diarrhoea. Some people are so allergic to nuts or other food, their bodies can go into **extreme shock** if they eat them. People who are likely to react like this usually carry medicine that will help them to recover quickly.

If you are allergic to nuts or any other kind of food, you have to check the ingredients on the label before you eat anything.

Skin reaction

Food **allergies** do not affect only the **digestive system**. The most common sign of a food allergy is an itchy rash. Many people who are allergic to strawberries, shellfish and nuts come out in a rash or angry red blotches when they eat them. A food allergy can also make it difficult for some people to breathe.

This girl cannot eat anything that has cheese in it. Cheese makes her irritable and stops her from sleeping.

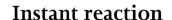

Instant reaction

Many people react very quickly to a food they are allergic to. Within minutes their skin breaks out in a rash, or they feel sick, or their mouth swells up. If this happens, it is fairly easy to tell what has caused the reaction. Other people take longer to react. If you are sick three days after eating something, you may not realize the cause.

Food can affect other conditions

A food allergy may trigger **eczema**, an **asthma** attack or other conditions, such as migraine. A migraine is a very bad headache, but many people also vomit or feel dizzy. They may see wiggly lines or dots in front of their eyes. Different things cause migraines in different people, but many migraine sufferers find that eating cheese, or chocolate, or a chemical called monosodium glutamate (often listed as E621) triggers an attack.

COMMON FOOD ALLERGIES:

- peanuts and other nuts
- strawberries, tomatoes
- milk, cheese, yoghurt
- chocolate
- wheat
- fish or shellfish
- pork
- monosodium glutamate (used in crisps, Chinese food and many other foods)
- medicines, particularly penicillin and aspirin.

Eating strawberries, shellfish or other foods can cause a rash like this. It may only last a few hours but is very uncomfortable.

CAN FOOD ALLERGIES BE CURED?

An **allergy** cannot be cured, but it can go away. Many young children grow out of allergies. If you are allergic to cheese, for example, the allergy may disappear when you are older. Or, if you avoid eating cheese for several months, your body may become less **sensitive** to cheese. If you have one or more allergies, there are several things you can do to reduce their effect.

Avoiding allergens

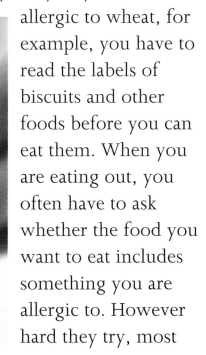

This girl is taking a drug that includes **antihistamine**. It will allow her to eat some foods she is allergic to.

If you are allergic to something, it is best to avoid it. This is not always easy. If you are allergic to wheat, for example, you have to read the labels of biscuits and other foods before you can eat them. When you are eating out, you often have to ask whether the food you want to eat includes something you are allergic to. However hard they try, most

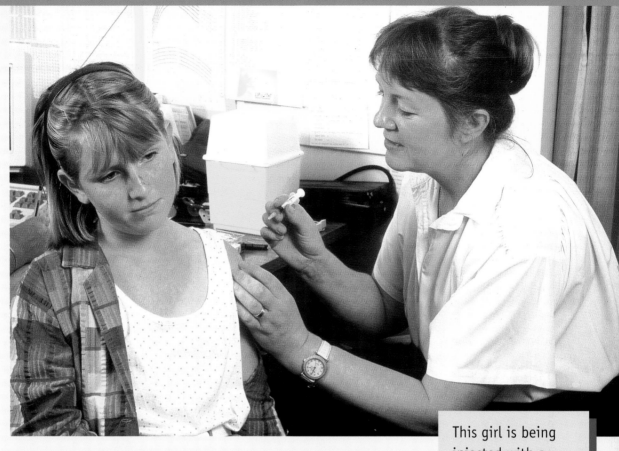

This girl is being injected with a tiny amount of the food she is allergic to. As the dose is increased, her body becomes used to the food and no longer reacts against it.

people who are allergic to some kind of food eat it by mistake from time to time.

A little at a time

Some people who are allergic to foods can eat them, so long as they do not eat too much of them too often. A few people become allergic to more and more different foods. They have to be very careful. They eat a few kinds of food for four or five days, and then they eat different foods for the next four or five days. In this way, they hope that their bodies will accept the foods.

HOW DO DOCTORS TEST FOR ALLERGIES?

It is sometimes difficult to work out what is causing an **allergy**. You may be able to detect the culprit (what is responsible) yourself or you may need the help of an allergy clinic.

This girl is being given a prick test to find out what she is allergic to. She may be allergic to more than one allergen.

Detecting the culprit

If your skin suddenly develops an allergic rash, try to remember whether you recently used a new cream or soap. Some allergies develop slowly, so an old cream could be the cause. If you cannot find the **allergen**, stop using everything that it could be. If the rash goes away, then start using the creams again, but reintroduce them one at a time. You should then discover the culprit. Doctors sometimes use the same method to detect the cause of food allergies.

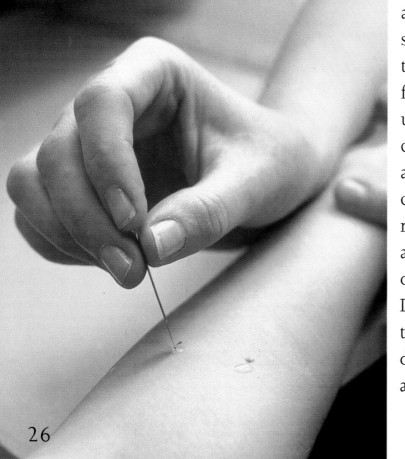

26

Skin prick test

If you are allergic to something that affects your breathing system, an allergy clinic may use a skin prick test to find out the allergens. Tiny amounts of different allergens are dropped onto your skin. Any allergens that make your skin react are the culprits.

Blood test

Sometimes the clinic can find the allergens by testing a small sample of your blood. They look for particular **antibodies** in the blood. If you are allergic to pollen, for example, your blood will have antibodies against it.

Being allergic is often inherited, but not the allergy itself. All the members of this family suffer from a different allergy.

Inheriting allergies

Allergies often run in families. If one parent has an allergy, then one child out of three will probably have an allergy too. If both parents have allergies, then two or even three children out of three will probably have an allergy.

ARE ALLERGIES DANGEROUS?

Most allergies are not dangerous, but if an allergy leads to **extreme shock** then it is dangerous. Extreme shock is also called anaphylactic shock. It can happen very quickly and involves the whole body.

Extreme shock

The person's lips, tongue and face swell up and they sometimes look very pale. They find it difficult to breathe and become unconscious. The person's blood pressure becomes very low. If they do not receive medical help at once, they will die. A doctor can inject drugs to reduce swelling and increase their blood pressure. Oxygen helps them to breathe normally. The most common causes of extreme shock are bee and wasp stings, nuts, shellfish, eggs and antibiotics.

This woman is enjoying a meal of seafood. If she is allergic to shellfish, she should not risk eating it because shellfish can cause extreme shock.

BODY MAP

Mucus washes dirt, germs and allergens from the nose

Tears wash dirt and other irritants from the eye

Saliva helps to kill some germs

Fine hairs and mucus push dirt, germs and allergens from breathing tubes

Stomach muscles push out poisonous food and allergens when you vomit

White cells and antibodies in the blood kill germs

Histamine allows blood to flood damaged areas of the body

GLOSSARY

allergen   something that causes an allergy

allergy   when the body reacts to something as though it were a germ, although the same thing is harmless to most people

antibodies   special cells carried in the blood that attack particular germs or allergens

antihistamine   a medicine that blocks the effects of histamine

asthma   a condition in which the breathing tubes become narrow, making it difficult to breathe

biological detergents   washing powders and liquids that can contain enzymes (special chemicals) that eat up dirt in clothes

bronchial tubes   tubes that carry air in and out of the lungs

cell   the smallest building block of living things. The body has many kinds of cells, including lung cells and skin cells.

digestive system   the parts of the body involved with digesting food

eczema   a condition that causes dry, itchy skin, sometimes with small spots and blisters

extreme shock an extreme life-threatening reaction to an allergen

germs tiny living things that can make you ill

histamine chemical made by the body when part of the body is damaged or when antibodies detect a germ or allergen

mucus slime that coats the inside of parts of the body, including the nose and bronchial tubes

sensitive easily affected by

synthetic materials materials, such as plastic, nylon and polythene, that are made from oil

FURTHER READING

First Encylopedia of the Human Body, 2001, Kingfisher Books

I know how to fight germs, Kate Rowan, 2000, Walker Books

The Human Body Big Book, Penny Coltman, 1999, Longman

Young Discoverers: Inside the Body, Sally Morgan, 1997, Kingfisher

INDEX

Titles in the *Body Matters* series include:

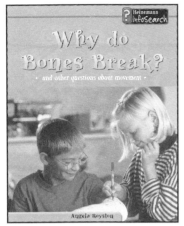

Hardback   0431 11075 1

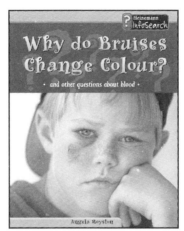

Hardback   0431 11073 5

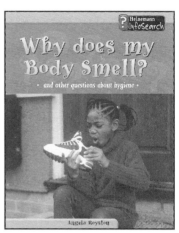

Hardback   0431 11077 8

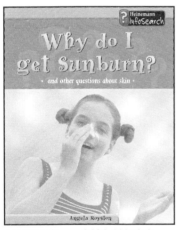

Hardback   0431 11078 6

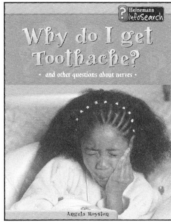

Hardback   0431 11076 X

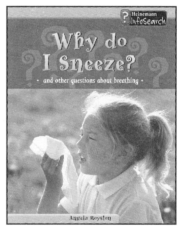

Hardback   0431 11070 0

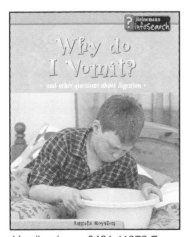

Hardback   0431 11072 7

Hardback   0431 11071 9

Find out about the other titles in this series on our website www.heinemann.co.uk/library